INSTRUMENTAL PLAY-ALONG

AUDIO ACCESS INCLUDED

PLAYBACK+
Speed · Pitch · Balance · Loop

ALTO SAX

SUPERHERO THEMES

T0086982

Audio arrangements by Peter Deneff

To access audio, visit:
www.halleonard.com/mylibrary

Enter Code
7222-9561-5255-1446

ISBN 978-1-70513-160-2

Visit Hal Leonard Online at
www.halleonard.com

Contact us:
Hal Leonard
7777 West Bluemound Road
Milwaukee, WI 53213
Email: info@halleonard.com

In Europe, contact:
Hal Leonard Europe Limited
42 Wigmore Street
Marylebone, London, W1U 2RN
Email: info@halleonardeurope.com

In Australia, contact:
Hal Leonard Australia Pty. Ltd.
4 Lentara Court
Cheltenham, Victoria, 3192 Australia
Email: info@halleonard.com.au

THEME FROM ANT-MAN
from MARVEL'S ANT-MAN

ALTO SAX

Music by CHRISTOPHE BECK

WAKANDA
from BLACK PANTHER

Music by LUDWIG GÖRANSSON

THE AVENGERS
from THE AVENGERS

ALTO SAX

Composed by
ALAN SILVESTRI

BATMAN THEME

ALTO SAX

Words and Music by
NEAL HEFTI

CAPTAIN AMERICA MARCH

from CAPTAIN AMERICA

ALTO SAX

By ALAN SILVESTRI

ELASTIGIRL IS BACK

from INCREDIBLES 2

ALTO SAX

Composed by
MICHAEL GIACCHINO

IMMORTALS
from BIG HERO 6

ALTO SAX

Words and Music by ANDREW HURLEY,
JOE TROHMAN, PATRICK STUMP
and PETE WENTZ

GUARDIANS INFERNO
from GUARDIANS OF THE GALAXY VOL. 2

ALTO SAX

Words and Music by JAMES GUNN
and TYLER BATES

THE INCREDITS
from THE INCREDIBLES

ALTO SAX

Music by MICHAEL GIACCHINO

POW! POW! POW! - MR. INCREDIBLES THEME

from INCREDIBLES 2

ALTO SAX

Music and Lyrics by
MICHAEL GIACCHINO

IRON MAN
from IRON MAN

ALTO SAX

By RAMIN DJAWADI

ROCKETEER END TITLES

from THE ROCKETEER

ALTO SAX

By JAMES HORNER

THEME FROM SPIDER MAN

ALTO SAX

Written by BOB HARRIS
and PAUL FRANCIS WEBSTER

X-MEN: APOCALYPSE - END TITLES

from X-MEN: APOCALYPSE

ALTO SAX

By JOHN OTTMAN